What C

Susan Vaughan

Rosen Real Readers

Rosen Classroom Books & Materials
New York

I have $1.00. What can I buy?

I can buy a ball.

I can buy some cookies.

I can buy an apple.

I can buy some crayons.

What other things can I buy?

Words to Know

apple

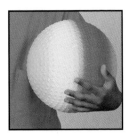

ball

cookies

crayons